BIBLE STUDY LEADER COURSE WORKBOOK

Learning to lead with confidence & grace

By Melanie Newton

This workbook coordinates with the E-Course, *Bible Study Leadership Made Easy*, by Melanie Newton. Access this E-course through melanienewton.com/courses.

© 2017 Melanie Newton | Joyful Walk Ministries

All rights reserved.

This workbook coordinates with the E-Course, *Bible Study Leadership Made Easy*, by Melanie Newton. Access this E-course through melanienewton.com/courses.

Permission is granted to reproduce pages for personal use but not for resale. For any other questions about the use of this course workbook, please visit melanienewton.com to contact us.

Cover design and study layout by Melanie Newton.

Published by Joyful Walk Ministries.

Scripture quotations indicated NIV are taken from the Holy Bible, New International Version ®, NIV ®. Copyright © 1973, 1978, 1984, 2011 by International Bible Society. Used by permission of Zondervan Publishing Company. All rights reserved.

Melanie Newton is a Lifestyle Disciplemaking speaker, author, and trainer with Joyful Walk Ministries. She is the author of *Graceful Beginnings* books for anyone new to the Bible and *Joyful Walk Bible Studies* for growing Christians. Melanie can be contacted at melanienewton.com.

We pray that you will find this *Bible Study Leadership Made Easy* workbook a resource that God will use to strengthen you in your own faith walk and in your Bible-teaching skills to help others grow in their faith.

JOYFUL WALK PRESS
Flower Mound, TX

In This Workbook

SECTION 1. BEGIN THE ADVENTURE — JUST SAY YES!   3

    Why You Can Do This…by Faith!   5

    "How to Choose a Bible Study" Checklist   7

    Getting Started Checklist   11

SECTION 2. STEP FORWARD AS THE LEADER   13

    First Day of Bible Study Checklist   15

    Sample Introduction and First Lesson   17

SECTION 3. PREPARE WISELY AS CONTENT GUARDIAN   23

    Lesson Leading Checklist   25

    Sample Lesson Leading Plan   27

SECTION 4. LEAD CONFIDENTLY AS CONTENT GUARDIAN   33

    Guidelines for the Content Guardian   35

    Work through a Lesson   37

    Lesson Plan Worksheet   43

SECTION 5. LEAD GRACIOUSLY AS COMMUNITY BUILDER   45

    Common Challenges Worksheet   47

SECTION 6. ENJOY THE ADVENTURE   51

    Resources Page   53

Welcome

Hey there. This is me, Melanie Newton, founder of Joyful Walk Ministries and author of *Joyful Walk Bible Studies* used by 1000s of people around the world to grow in their faith walk with Jesus Christ.

My passion is to help women learn how to study the Bible for themselves and to grow their Bible-teaching skills to help others—all with the goal of getting to know Jesus more and more along the way.

This workbook coordinates with my E-Course, *Bible Study Leadership Made Easy*. Access the E-course through melanienewton.com/courses.

I'm excited you're here right now because it means you're ready to lead a Bible Study for a group. Or, at least you are thinking about doing that. ☺

I get lots of emails from people who have chosen to do one of my *Joyful Walk Bible Studies* with their group. And, they usually ask this one big question, "How do I lead the discussion when we get together?" That may be your question as well. Be assured that you are not alone. That's why I'm here to help you.

Welcome to the course *Bible Study Leadership Made Easy*. This special course will teach you how to lead a Bible study with confidence and grace. *Bible Study Leadership Made Easy* is designed to get you moving forward as a new Bible study leader or to give you extra help if you already have some experience at leading a study for a group.

Through this course, you will learn how to put together a Bible study group, how to choose a good study for your group, and how to take each lesson and make a plan for leading the discussion. We will also address some common challenges that arise as you are leading a Bible study.

Watch the videos as many times as you want. Make copies of the worksheets and checklists to use over and over. These are resources for you to use as you grow your Bible-teaching skills to help others walk joyfully with Jesus.

I am excited about sharing with you some insights that have helped me over many years of leading women's small group Bible studies. I want to help you gain confidence to lead your group using any of my *Joyful Walk Bible* study books. But, the principles I share are transferrable to other Bible study guides as well. Are you ready for adventure? So, let's get started.

Living joyfully,

Melanie

SECTION 1:

Begin the Adventure – Just Say Yes!

MELANIE NEWTON

WHY YOU CAN DO THIS…BY FAITH!

You **CAN** lead a Bible Study…**BY FAITH**!

1. **Understand that faith is the essential component of the Christian life.**

   ➢ We are to live every day by faith. That is what Paul is communicating to us in Galatians.

   I have been crucified with Christ and I no longer live, but Christ lives in me. The life I now live in the body, I LIVE BY FAITH in the Son of God, who loved me and gave Himself for me. (Galatians 2:20)

   The life you and I live every day is by faith in the Son of God—Jesus Himself.

   Jesus Christ gave His life for you, so that He could give His life to you, so that He could live His life through you. (Ian Thomas, The Saving Life of Christ)

   ➢ If you are being prompted by the Lord to lead a Bible study, **just say yes – "I will do this, Lord. Please help me."** Jesus is with you every step of the way.

2. **Know that you can lead a Bible study—by faith:**

   ➢ You can do this by faith in your church, neighborhood, community, or workplace.

   ➢ You can do this by faith at any age or stage of life. Someone around you needs to know Jesus or to know Him better through studying the Bible.

   ➢ You can do this by faith with any size group—large or small.

   ➢ You can do this by faith whether you have been studying the Bible for 2 years or doing it for decades. Share what you know and what you are learning.

   ➢ You can do this by faith because whatever Jesus calls you to do, He enables you to do through His Spirit.

   You can lead a Bible study not because you are so great or smart or have been a Christian a long time or know the Bible really well. You can do this because Jesus is the one who enables you to do it. Say "yes" and jump in with both feet. **Step out in faith!**

3. **Desire the Benefits of leading a Bible study**

   Leading a Bible study can be one of the greatest adventures you've ever tried. And it's good for you. It has benefits for you. What are those benefits if you say yes to leading a Bible study?

   ➢ It **presses you to grow** and learn for yourself. You always learn more when you prepare to help someone else grow in their faith. Always.

   ➢ It teaches you how **to depend on Jesus Christ more**. And, whatever leads you to depend on Him is a good thing for you. We are to live by faith in Him and let Him live His life through us.

SECTION 1: YOU CAN DO THIS…BY FAITH

4. Trust Jesus with Your Insecurities

- Give your insecurities to Jesus. He is the one who makes you able to do everything in the Christian life, and that includes leading a Bible study. You are simply to obey Him and trust His Spirit to work through you.
- Being scared is a good thing – you will rely on Him more.
- It is okay to say, **"Lord, I can't do this on my own, but you can in me and through me. I will trust you with this."**

Write your insecurities and concerns about leading a Bible Study:

Give them to Jesus and say, "Yes, Lord. I will trust you with these."

And then, watch what He does! Go ahead, begin the adventure.

HAVE YOU SAID, "YES?" YIPPEE!

SIGN UP FOR MY E-COURSE AT MELANIENEWTON.COM/COURSES. GET ACCESS TO ALL THE VIDEOS I OFFER TO HELP YOU BE THE BEST BIBLE STUDY LEADER YOU CAN BE.

MELANIE NEWTON

"HOW TO CHOOSE A BIBLE STUDY" CHECKLIST

Ask Jesus to help you with all of the following steps to choosing a Bible study for your group. Depend on Him to show you what to do. He is faithful!

☐ **CHOOSE A BIBLE STUDY NOT A POPULAR BOOK STUDY**

➢ Look for a prepared Bible Study that covers portions of the Bible (whole books or sections of the Bible) in an organized fashion. These workbooks or study guides are scripted to help you learn by reading the Bible verse(s) then answering specific questions based on what you just read.

➢ Look for a Bible study workbook that focuses more on what you are learning from your study of the Bible passages than on reading commentary from the author.

➢ Look at the format of the study. Can the questions be used as a guide for leading the discussion? A well-written Bible Study guide will make it easier for you to learn how to lead a Bible Study.

➢ *Don't choose a popular book containing some Bible verses in it* that may have a leader's guide in the back. That is not a Bible study. Those can be valuable learning tools but not as a Bible study.

All of my *Joyful Walk Bible Studies* are prepared Bible Studies.

☐ **CHOOSE AN "INDUCTIVE BIBLE STUDY"**

There are two methods of Bible Study —inductive and deductive.

➢ The **Induction Method** follows three steps: observation, interpretation and application. The process is more easily understood by answering three questions:

   1) What does the passage say? (Observation: what's actually there)

   2) What does it mean? (Interpretation: the author's intended meaning for his/her audience)

   3) How do I live this out in my life? (Application: making it personal)

This is the best way to study the Bible. Look at what's there. Learn what it means and teaches you. Then, live it out in your life.

➢ The **Deductive Method** starts with a topic or theme then looks for verses in the Bible that match what you are wanting to know. There are two cautions about using this method of Bible study:

   • *Caution #1:* This method can be used to selectively choose Bible verses to prove anything that someone wants to prove.

   • *Caution #2:* This method feeds the "look-imagine-see" way of looking at the Bible. One *looks* at a verse or passages, *imagines* what they want it to say, and then *sees* what they have imagined. Many types of false teaching have started with this kind of "look-imagine-see" process.

SECTION 1: "HOW TO CHOOSE A BIBLE STUDY" CHECKLIST

The deductive method is not a reliable method for studying the Bible. Be aware that sometimes popular topics use this method. Check the front of the study guide to see if it says it follows the inductive process.

All of my *Joyful Walk Bible Studies* on melanienewton.com are "Inductive Bible Studies."

☐ **CONSIDER THE TIME ALLOTTED FOR THE GROUP TO MEET**

- Do you have 1½ to 2 hours? You can usually cover one lesson per session without rushing through the lesson.

- Do you have only an hour or less? Choose a shorter study or a study that can be divided into two sessions. You don't want to feel rushed trying to get through all of the questions in a short time. You want the group time to be a learning experience, not just a challenge to get through it.

☐ **CONSIDER THE SPIRITUAL MATURITY OF THE GROUP**

- **Will your group members be mostly those new to the Bible?**

  - Look for a Bible study designed for those who are new to the Bible or beginners at studying the Bible.

  - Look for basic lessons with simple questions and applications that are easy-to-understand for beginners.

  - *Graceful Beginnings* studies are designed for anyone new to the Bible.

"GRACEFUL BEGINNINGS" STUDIES

✓ Are they mostly new Christians? Start with **A Fresh Start**. This will give you confidence that you are heading in the right direction.

✓ Do they need to get to know Jesus better? **Painting the Portrait of Jesus** covers what Jesus says about Himself in the gospel of John.

✓ Do they need to know more about the character of God? **The God You Can Know** teaches them to trust God as your loving Father.

✓ Do they deal with a lot of fear? **The Walk from Fear to Faith** teaches them to trust God with their fears.

✓ Do they feel lost understanding how a lot of the New Testament fits together? **Grace Overflowing** gives an overview of all of Paul's letters and how each teaches something special about Jesus.

✓ Do they need to have confidence in Jesus' love? **Satisfied by His Love** is a new study that affirms Jesus' love in your life.

SECTION 1: "HOW TO CHOOSE A BIBLE STUDY" CHECKLIST

- ➤ **Will your group members already have some experience studying the Bible?** You have lots of options. Just make sure they follow the Inductive Bible Study Method as described above. Consider *Joyful Walk Bible Studies* for growing Christians.

"JOYFUL WALK BIBLE STUDIES"

- ✓ Are they dealing with a lot of fears in their lives, or do they need perseverance to face challenges with strong faith? Two Old Testament studies are particularly good for this. **Everyday Women, Ever-Faithful God** (Old Testament women) and **Profiles of Perseverance** (Old Testament men).

- ✓ Have they been in church for a while but still don't understand all that Jesus did for them? Work through the **Graceful Living** study to learn the daily benefits of Jesus' death and resurrection as well as your new identity in Christ, freeing you to live a new life with confidence and joy.

- ✓ Do they need to get a good handle on God as creator and sustainer? **The 7 C's of a Firm Foundation** takes you through Genesis 1-11 thoroughly and includes competent scientific and historical information that supports what the Bible actually says.

- ✓ Are they needing some joy in their lives? **Knowing Jesus...Knowing Joy!** Is a study of the book of Philippians.

- ✓ Are they looking for adventure with a purpose? Work through **Radical Acts** (the book of Acts) or **Live Out His Love** (New Testament women) which will prepare you to share your faith with others around you.

- ✓ Are they surrounded by false teaching and need to hang on firmly to truth? Work through **Healthy Living** (Colossians and Philemon), **Adorn Yourself with Godliness** (1 Timothy and Titus), or **Perspective** (1 & 2 Thessalonians).

- ✓ Are they thinking about growing old and how to stay faithful to Jesus as they do so? **To Be Found Faithful** would be perfect for that.

☐ **CHOOSE SOMETHING THAT INTERESTS YOU AND WILL GROW YOU IN YOUR FAITH**

- ➤ **What would be the best focus for you in your life right now or for your group?** Consider what you have already studied and what might be the best thing to build onto that. Choose your Bible study based on these.

- ➤ **What will make you passionate about the study so that you will want to dig in and learn for yourself?** It's important that you feed yourself from the Word of God before you try to lead others in a discussion. And, the joy of what you are learning will be infectious to those in your group.

- ➤ If you are putting together a new group, it's best for you to just choose the study and run with it rather than trying to please everyone in the group.

SECTION 1: "HOW TO CHOOSE A BIBLE STUDY" CHECKLIST

☐ **BE CAREFUL ABOUT CHOOSING A VIDEO-DRIVEN STUDY**

You can always learn something from gifted Bible teachers. But, when it comes to choosing a Bible Study for yourself or for your group, here are some questions to ask and things to consider before choosing a study that requires watching a video to complete it:

➤ **Does the study lead everyone to dig into the Bible for themselves to learn?**

- Is the personal Bible study time actual study of the Bible according to the inductive process or does it contain mostly thought and reflection questions?
- Can someone learn from the Bible passage through the study without watching the video at all? If yes, sounds like it might be a good study. If no, avoid it.

➤ **Will the cost for purchasing the videos and books be easily shared by the group members?**

- Video-driven studies are convenient but can be expensive. You must still purchase a workbook for every participant plus buy access to the videos.

➤ **Will the technology be a frustration for you?**

- You must depend on technology to work perfectly every time. Will that be a challenge for you? Will it fluster you if showing the video doesn't work during your group time?

➤ **Will watching the videos limit group interaction if time is short? Or, can group members watch the videos on their own?**

- It is very hard to find a video-driven study that can be used in an hour or less during a typical lunch hour at work or during an evening study at the end of a hard work day. The videos are generally too long to allow for much group discussion at all.
- It's hard to build community when you are just watching someone else talk. And, watching a video together is not a good substitute for interaction within the group.
- Can the group members watch the videos on their own time through an app or website and then share what they learned during group time? This is the better way when it comes to building community within the time limits that you have.

➤ **As leader, will you feel restricted to focus your discussion on whatever is taught in the video?**

- It is better if you can focus on what your particular group needs the most from the study.
- Again, look at the personal study portion to see if it covers the passage well.

The video should be like "icing on the cake" not the cake itself.

WANT TO CHECK OUT ALL OF MELANIE'S BIBLE STUDIES?

Go to melanienewton.com/free-bible-studies.

MELANIE NEWTON

GETTING STARTED CHECKLIST

Ask Jesus to help you with all of the following steps to starting a Bible study group. Depend on Him to show you what to do. He is faithful!

☐ CHOOSE A BIBLE STUDY GUIDE

- ➢ *Will your group be mostly those new to the Bible?* "GRACEFUL BEGINNINGS" studies are designed for those new to the Bible. The lessons are simple and easy-to-understand for beginners.

- ➢ *Will your group be mostly those with Bible Study experience?* "JOYFUL WALK BIBLE STUDIES" are for growing Christians who already have some experience studying the Bible.

- ➢ Follow the "HOW TO CHOOSE A BIBLE STUDY TO LEAD" CHECKLIST in this workbook to help you choose a quality Bible Study guide based on your interest, the group's Bible study experience, and your available group time. Your passion about the study will be infectious to your group.

☐ CHOOSE A TIME TO MEET

- ➢ Morning, lunch, afternoon, evening—what will work best for you and for those you invite?
- ➢ 1 hour, 1½ hours, 2 hours?
- ➢ Every week, every other week? For consistency, it is best to meet at least twice a month.

☐ FIND A PLACE TO MEET

- ➢ Church, school, office building—check to see if you must reserve a room
- ➢ Coffee shop, restaurant—you'll want to be able to hear and see each other
- ➢ Someone's home—consider a backup location

☐ SET A START DATE AND INVITE OTHERS TO JOIN YOU

☐ GET THE BIBLE STUDY BOOKS

- ➢ *Option 1:* Download and print for all the group members.
- ➢ *Option 2:* Order books for all the group members from Amazon.com.
- ➢ *Option 3:* Give the link for each member to order her own book

WOOHOO! THE ADVENTURE BEGINS!

SECTION 1: GETTING STARTED CHECKLIST

Sign up for my E-Course at melanienewton.com/courses. Get access to all the videos I offer to help you be the best Bible Study Leader you can be.

Section 2:

Step Forward as The Leader

MELANIE NEWTON

FIRST DAY OF BIBLE STUDY CHECKLIST

Ask Jesus to help you with all of the following steps to leading a Bible study group. Depend on Him to show you what to do. He is faithful!

There are two basic roles of a Bible Study group leader.

- ✓ Role #1: Content Guardian (guarding how the truth from God's Word is presented and received)
- ✓ Role #2: Community Builder (built around shared study and application of God's Word)

Those two roles are totally interlinked. As Content Guardian for your group, you have the authority to control the content of the Bible Study discussion. As Community Builder for your group, you have the privilege of managing the group interaction to help them love one another well. You as the leader set the tone for both of those roles the first time you get together.

1. Make a positive first impression

- ☐ Make sure that everyone can see and hear you and, if possible, see each other. Make adjustments to chairs and tables and where you sit to make this happen.
- ☐ Face the entrance to the room when you choose where to sit. If someone comes late, you can quickly give a welcome smile and even a wave to let them know you are happy to see them.
- ☐ Get acquainted with general questions, something that all the members have in common.
  - *Share name, what brought you to this study, how long have you lived in the area, favorite color to wear, favorite flower—just generic questions.*
  - *Avoid things like "tell us about your family" or "tell us about your job." You can share about those later as you get to know one another better. Introduce yourself and start.*
  - *Make this a "Whoever wants to go next" activity. You will build community more effectively if you let people respond when they feel ready to do so.*
- ☐ Find out the best way to communicate with each one—text, email, Facebook, phone call.
  - *Get their contact information if you don't have it, and let them know your contact information.*
  - *Give your group permission to contact you if they don't understand what a question is asking*
- ☐ Ask if anyone is new to studying the Bible.
  - *Make sure everyone has a Bible.*
  - *Make a note to yourself that those new to Bible Study might need help learning how to find Bible verses and answer questions.*
- ☐ Make sure everyone has a Bible Study book or knows where to get one.
  - *For anyone who misses the first day, get her book to her before the next meeting.*
- ☐ Pray for the group to learn from Jesus what He wants them to know and to learn how to love one another well.

SECTION 2: FIRST DAY OF BIBLE STUDY CHECKLIST

2. **Introduce the Study to generate interest**

    The following is based on the "Introduction" section found in most Joyful Walk Bible Studies.

    - [ ] Look at the "Contents" page and the number of lessons. Will you do one lesson per group time or take two sessions to do one lesson?
    - [ ] Look at the "Introduction" section and talk about the process of Bible Study. The best Bible Studies use the Inductive Method: Observation (What does the passage say?), Interpretation (What was the author's intended meaning?), and Application (How does this apply to me today?).
    - [ ] Go over the discussion group guidelines for your group. You can use the suggested ones in the study guide or add your own.
    - [ ] Tell them when you will start the group so they will know. And, be faithful about this.
    - [ ] Talk about how you will share prayer requests—in the group, individually given to you as leader then emailed to group members, and what to do about private requests.
    - [ ] Read through any Old Testament or New Testament summaries together.
    - [ ] Read through any explanation about the theme of the study.
    - [ ] Cover the ABCs—Author, Background and Context—for Bible studies that cover a specific book of the Bible.

3. **Walk through the first lesson to demonstrate how to do it**

    - [ ] Look at how the lesson is arranged. Point out the different parts of the lesson, if applicable.
    - [ ] If you have enough time, you can begin to do the lesson together. This demonstrates how to work through questions by reading the verses and answering the question.
    - [ ] If you get through part of the lesson, ask them to finish the rest of it at home. Otherwise, remind them to work on all of Lesson One at home before you get together again the next time.
    - [ ] Offer to help anyone new to the Bible
        - Tell those new to Bible study that if they have any questions about the lesson to contact you.
        - If you have several new women and several experienced at Bible studies, ask the experienced ones to partner with the new ones during the week, getting together to work the lesson.
    - [ ] Pray: ask Jesus to teach you what He wants you all to learn through this study. Commit your time and your personal Bible study time to Him. Say yes to this adventure together.

    Your journey together begins!

USE THIS CHECKLIST TO PRACTICE GOING THROUGH THE "SAMPLE INTRODUCTION AND FIRST LESSON" THAT FOLLOWS THIS PAGE.

MELANIE NEWTON

SAMPLE INTRODUCTION AND FIRST LESSON

Everyday Women, Ever-Faithful God

Introduction

This study guide consists of 11 lessons arranged chronologically according to Old Testament history. For those who are not familiar with the history of Israel found in the Old Testament, each lesson begins with a brief history of a particular time period and then covers the lives of 1-2 women who lived during that time.

The lessons are divided into 4 sections (about 20 minutes in length). The first 3 sections contain a detail study of the passages. The fourth section asks you to reflect on what you've learned. The goal is to help you establish a regular time of study in the Word for 5 days each week, considering your small group session to be one of those days. If you cannot do the entire lesson one week, please read the Bible passage being covered.

THE BASIC STUDY

Each lesson includes core questions covering the narrative associated with the lives of 1-2 women. These core questions will take you through the process of inductive Bible study—observation, interpretation, and application. The process is more easily understood in the context of answering these questions:

- What does the passage say? (Observation: what's actually there)
- What does it mean? (Interpretation: the author's intended meaning)
- How does this apply to me today? (Application: making it personal) **Your Life's Journey** questions lead you to introspection and application of a specific truth to your life.

STUDY ENHANCEMENTS

Deeper Discoveries (optional): Embedded within the sections are *optional* questions for further research of subjects we don't have time to cover adequately in the lessons or contain information that may enhance the basic study. If you are meeting with a small group, your leader may give you the opportunity to share your "discoveries."

Study Aids: To aid in proper interpretation and application of the study, additional study aids are located where appropriate in the lesson:

- Historical Insights
- Scriptural Insights
- From the Hebrew (definitions of Hebrew words)
- Focus on the Meaning
- Think About It (thoughtful reflection)

TELL YOUR STORY

This study is about the faith walk of women—those who lived in years past and those who live in the present. The scripture passages tell each Old Testament woman's "story" about her trust in God's faithfulness and goodness. Through **TELL YOUR STORY** questions in each lesson, you will be encouraged to write parts of your own story that relate to what's learned in the lesson. At the end of the study, you'll have enough information to put together a "My Story" of your own faith walk with God—especially your walk from fear to faith.

SECTION 2: SAMPLE INTRODUCTION AND FIRST LESSON

DISCUSSION GROUP GUIDELINES

1. **Attend consistently** whether your lesson is done or not. You'll learn from the other women, and they want to get to know you.

2. **Set aside time** to work through the study questions. The goal of Bible study is to **get to know** Jesus. He will change your life.

3. **Share your insights** from your personal study time. As you spend time in the Bible, Jesus will teach you truth through His Spirit inside you.

4. **Respect each other's insights**. Listen thoughtfully. Encourage each other as you interact. Refrain from dominating the discussion if you have a tendency to be talkative. ☺

5. **Celebrate our unity** in Christ. Avoid bringing up controversial subjects such as politics, divisive issues, and denominational differences.

6. **Maintain confidentiality.** Remember that anything shared during the group time is not to leave the **group** (unless permission is granted by the one sharing).

7. **Pray for one another** as sisters in Christ.

8. **Get to know the women** in your group. Please do not use your small group members for solicitation purposes for home businesses, though.

OLD TESTAMENT SUMMARY

About 1700 years after God created everything, He sent judgment on a rebellious race through a worldwide Flood. He later separated the nations with different languages and scattered them from Babel. Abraham, Isaac, and Jacob were founding fathers of the Hebrew people. Sold into slavery, Joseph became a powerful foreign leader. The Israelites grew in number for ~400 years in Egypt. Then God delivered them from bondage through Moses who took the people across the Red Sea and taught them God's Law at Mt. Sinai. Joshua led the Israelites into the Promised Land after a 40-year trek in the wilderness because of unbelief.

During the transition toward monarchy, there were deliverer-rulers called "Judges," the last of whom was Samuel. The first three Hebrew kings—Saul, David, and Solomon—each ruled 40 years. Under Rehoboam, the Hebrew nation divided into northern and southern kingdoms, respectively called Israel and Judah. Prophets warned against worshipping the foreign god Baal. After the reign of 19 wicked kings in the north, Assyria conquered and scattered the northern kingdom. In the south, 20 kings ruled for ~350 years, until Babylon took the people into captivity for 70 years. Zerubbabel, Ezra, and Nehemiah led the Jews back into Jerusalem over a 100-year period. More than 400 "silent years" spanned the gap between Malachi and Matthew.

The 39 books in the Old Testament are divided into 4 main categories:

- "The Law" (5 books)—the beginning of the nation of Israel as God's chosen people; God giving His Laws to the people that made them distinct from the rest of the nations.

- "HISTORY" (12 books)—narratives that reveal what happened from the time the people entered the Promised Land right after Moses died until 400 years before Christ was born.

- "POETRY & WISDOM" (5 books)—take place at the same time as the history books but are set apart because they are written as poems and have a lot of wise teaching in them.

SECTION 2: SAMPLE INTRODUCTION AND FIRST LESSON

- "PROPHETS" (17 books)—concurrent with the books of history and, except for Lamentations, reflect the name of the prophet through whom God spoke to the nation of Israel.

TRUSTING AN EVER-FAITHFUL GOD

This study examines the faith walk of women who lived in Old Testament days. Like many women today, you may have very little knowledge of the Old Testament. You might look at that half of your Bible and think, "What's written in it happened so long ago—anywhere from 2-4 thousand years ago. What do those women have in common with *me*? They don't live in *my* world. They seem just like names on a page."

If you like to read biographies, doesn't reading someone's story make that person come alive for you? Or, you may have done genealogy work on your family tree. It can be great to find something to brag about. But, you can also find out some of your ancestors' dark secrets and hardships. I don't know about you, but I feel a connection to that great-great grandmother when I learn a little bit about her life. Hopefully, that's what you will experience through this study.

These Old Testament women were **EVERYDAY WOMEN**, just like we are, with many of the same experiences and challenges that we have. We'll see an **EVER-FAITHFUL GOD** in action—a faithful God whose character never changes. He's as faithful now in our everyday circumstances of life as He was years ago to them. We can feel confidence in His presence and active involvement, even when we can't see it. And, knowing this, we can trust in Him whenever we are afraid. And, we are often afraid, aren't we?

A few years ago, I heard Jill Briscoe say, "Women are a fear-driven, performance-oriented species." I think she's right. Fear is an ever-present emotion with us. Real fears and imagined fears. Is it realistic to think we can live without fear? No! Fear is a normal human emotion designed by God to alert us to danger so that we will take action against it. Yet, fear can take root in us and cause us to give way to panic and hysteria. God knows this about us. When we are afraid, God wants us to trust Him and not give way to fear. Learning to do so is our **WALK FROM FEAR TO FAITH**.

As we join these Old Testament women on their walk from fear to faith, we will see consistent truths that we can apply to our lives today in our faith walk…

- ➤ God loves me.
- ➤ God knows what is going on in my life.
- ➤ God can do something about it.
- ➤ I can trust His goodness in whatever He chooses to do!

Your walk from fear to faith begins as you count on these truths and live each day believing they are true.

Your faith walk is your story, your biography of God's faithfulness to you and your response back to Him. Each one of these women had a story, and that story has been shared over and over to millions of eager listeners. You're going to get to know it as you get to know them. It's a connection with real women, **EVERYDAY WOMEN**.

And, each one of you has a story. You will be given opportunities throughout the study to recall parts of your story, write about it, and share it with others. And, you'll have more reason to praise our **EVER-FAITHFUL** God as you see and hear how He has been faithful to each of you through the years. It's going to be a great journey. And, I'm so glad to be walking beside you!

SECTION 2: SAMPLE INTRODUCTION AND FIRST LESSON

Everyday Women, Ever-Faithful God Bible Study

Lesson 1: The Walk from Fear to Faith

(This sample contains only the first section of the lesson.)

Time Period: Creation through today

> *"When I am afraid, I will trust in you. In God, whose word I praise, in God I trust; I will not be afraid. What can mortal man do to me?"* PSALM 56:3-4

The Gift of Fear

You know that feeling. The pit in your stomach, pounding of your heart, and rush of your thoughts as you go from just the possibility of a job loss to starving and being homeless on the streets—all in a matter of seconds. Gripped by fear, although an imagined one.

Fear is a normal human emotion designed by God to alert us to danger so that we will take action against it. It has a purpose. It tells us to take precautions, to be wise in our dealings with strangers and strange situations. We need to think of it as a gift.

We know fear has a dark side as well. Bible teacher Jill Briscoe has often said, "Women are a fear-driven, performance-oriented species." Just watching the daily news can panic us. What did she mean by fear-driven? Why would fear drive us? And, what does fear drive us to do?

Women in general are created with a nesting instinct, a need for security and stability, and a desire to control our environment in order to create that security for us and for those we love. Our American way of thinking is this: we can fix it—whatever IT is. When we cannot fix it, we panic. And, fear can bring out the worst in us, especially in our uncertain world rife with the threat of terrorism. The damaging effect of constant fear is a disorienting sense that no place is safe.

Fear can be real or imagined. For me, a real fear is meeting a snake in my woodsy yard while gardening. I know they are there so I carefully do everything I can to avoid interaction with them. I experienced an imagined fear as my youngest daughter was growing up. That fear manifested itself in ongoing nightmares about her being kidnapped or molested. She was never threatened that way, but she was friendly and outgoing. I guess I thought she was more vulnerable than my older, more cautious daughter. When that young daughter became a strong teen girl who was daily hockey-checking her older brother into the wall as they met each other in the hallway, those nightmares stopped. I guess my subconscious recognized that she could handle herself.

Is it realistic to think we can live without fear? No! Our faithful God understands this about us. He doesn't want us to stay there, disoriented and hopeless. He gives us the answer—Himself!

DAY ONE STUDY

1. Read Psalm 56:3-4. Write out these verses in the space provided below.

2. Reading back over those words you just wrote, underline the phrases that tell you what to do when you are afraid. Then, write them below.

SECTION 2: SAMPLE INTRODUCTION AND FIRST LESSON

Notice that David doesn't write, "**If** I am afraid." He says, "**When** I am afraid." Fear will happen. We can let fear take root in us so that we give way to panic and hysteria. Does that ring any bells with you? Are you prone to hysterics? God knows this about us. When we are afraid, God wants us to trust Him and not give way to fear. Learning to do that is your walk from fear to faith.

Since God understands the tendency to fear and panic in us, the Holy Spirit inspired Peter to write encouragement and instructions to women in 1 Peter 3:3-6.

3. Read 1 Peter 3:3-6. What does God consider of great worth in His sight (verse 4)?

Although the context of this passage is a marriage relationship, the principles apply to any woman's character ("inner self"), especially the qualities of a GENTLE and QUIET spirit that are precious in God's sight. These enable a woman to "do what is right and not give way to fear" (verse 6). But, you may be thinking, "How can that apply to me? I have a bubbly personality. I'm not naturally quiet." Before you start feeling put out about these words or afraid that you could never measure up to this, let's find out what "gentle" and "quiet" actually mean.

> **Scriptural Insight:** "GENTLE" means **"controlled strength."** It does not mean passive, weak, or someone who cannot help herself. Picture a mother cradling a newborn. She has the physical strength to harm that child but doesn't because her strength is under control. If you are going to have a gentle spirit, what will you need? Strength under control. A woman with a gentle spirit has a humble heart that bows itself before God, recognizes God's dealings with her as good, and chooses not to be contentious or resistant against Him.
>
> "QUIET" means "tranquility arising from within." It does not mean whisper, silent, or bland. "Quiet" includes the idea of causing no disturbance to others. Think how a woman's hysterics affect those around her—family, friends, and coworkers. A woman with a quiet spirit has an inner peace and calmness in the midst of any circumstances. We can have a tranquil spirit in the midst of chaos. See how it fits with the "strength under control" attitude?

Gentleness and peace are fruits of the Holy Spirit (Gal. 5: 22-23) in a believer's life and available to every Christian woman who desires them—that includes you and me! Now that you know the real meanings of these words, are you more likely to desire these qualities?

4. Why do you think these qualities in a woman would be so precious – of great worth – to God?

5. Read 1 Peter 3:5-6 written below and underline the three choices women can make, identified by (1), (2), and (3).

> *"For this is the way the holy women of the past who (1) put their hope in God used to make themselves beautiful. They were submissive to their own husbands, like Sarah, who obeyed Abraham and called him her master. You are her daughters if you (2) do what is right and (3) do not give way to fear."*

Peter identifies these examples for us as "holy women of the past." The word "holy" means set apart for God's special use. These women are holy because they've learned to trust in God when they were afraid. As holy women, these women were beautiful in God's eyes (regardless of their outward appearance, age or social status). This beauty attributed to them by God Himself was based on three choices they made ("used to make themselves beautiful") that every woman can make today:

SECTION 2: SAMPLE INTRODUCTION AND FIRST LESSON

- Choice #1: You can put your hope in God—in God and His Word rather than the fickleness of ourselves or others.
- Choice #2: You can do what is right—according to God's way of approaching life, not the world's way, especially those cultural practices that go against God's Word.
- Choice #3: You can choose to not give way to fear. Let's examine this one more closely.

CHOOSE TO NOT GIVE WAY TO FEAR

What does that mean—not give way to fear? We know this: God is not saying, "Don't ever feel fear." God gave us the gift of fear as a normal human emotion designed to alert us to danger so we can take action against it. God is saying, "You don't have to stay terrified and paralyzed by your fear." We are to TRUST GOD—in whom we have put our hope and by whose Word we are taught to do what is right.

6. Have you ever felt terrified? How did you respond?

7. God says that having a gentle and quiet inner spirit will make it easier for us to not get so terrified and stay that way. What's harder for God: rescuing us from desperate circumstances or developing in us a gentle and quiet spirit? Why?

Did you select the "developing in us a gentle and quiet spirit?" I agree because it involves our cooperation! Is it too difficult for Him? No! But here's the key: a humble, peaceful heart makes it easier for us to make that choice to trust in the faithfulness of God rather than the fickleness of ourselves or others when we are tempted to panic and succumb to hysteria.

We have a faithful God. That's not imaginary. In 1 Peter 3:5, Sarah represents several other everyday women who lived in Old Testament days who put their hope in God and found Him worthy of their trust. This was their walk from fear to faith. What is that? We'll find out in the Day Two Study.

8. **Your Life's Journey:** What might be holding you back from trusting God whenever you are afraid?

> **Think About It:** "When we experience anxiety or fear, the enemy can try to use it as an opportunity to make us feel guilt or shame. That's when we pause and ask God for help, knowing He understands and never condemns us." (Holley Gerth, "Fear Not," Homelife Magazine, March 2016)

You're doing great. Keep going!

WANT TO READ OR WORK THROUGH THE REST OF THIS FIRST LESSON?

Go to melanienewton.com/ot-women.

Section 3:

Prepare Wisely as Content Guardian

MELANIE NEWTON

LESSON LEADING CHECKLIST

Ask Jesus to help you with all of the following steps to leading a Bible study group. Depend on Him to show you what to do. He is faithful!

1. Work through the lesson yourself

- [ ] Be a learner before being a teacher
- [ ] Enhance the study with what the Word teaches you
- [ ] Use good study aids to increase understanding, such as these online Bible Study tools:
    - www.Bible.org—get quality biblical research and commentary on a topic or passage
    - www.soniclight.com—Dr. Tom Constable's Study Notes (verse by verse commentary on every book of the Bible, free to download
    - www.blueletterbible.org—also the Blue Letter Bible app for phone or tablet; great for translation comparisons and original Hebrew and Greek word meanings

2. Review the lesson to plan how you will lead it

Go back over the lesson to develop a plan for leading the discussion. You are the content guardian for the group. Ask Jesus to help you make a plan. He will guide you through the Holy Spirit living inside you. *It's okay to say, "Lord Jesus, I can't do this on my own. I will trust you to do this through me."* Then, watch what He does!

- [ ] Consider how long your group gets to meet.
    - If you have a couple of hours, you can usually cover the whole lesson with time for creative discussion of the application questions.
    - If you have only an hour or less, choose which questions you want to discuss as a group. Or, split the lesson into two separate meeting times.
- [ ] Mark the Bible passages you will read in the group. Always read the main Bible passages that are the focus of the lesson.
- [ ] Mark the questions that could be combined together into one general discussion.
- [ ] Mark the questions that could be skipped without affecting the discussion.
- [ ] Mark anything that might be confusing or lead to extra discussion not related to the lesson (rabbit trails). Write yourself a "Watch out for this" note in the margin of the study.
- [ ] Decide how you will cover the application questions: as a large group, in smaller groups of 2-4, or skipped because too personal.
- [ ] Mark any optional *Deeper Discoveries* questions that would enhance the discussion.
- [ ] Include good follow-up questions you gained from your own study.

SECTION 3: LESSON LEADING CHECKLIST

3. Make a simple plan

Write a simple plan for covering the questions. If you have a tendency to forget details, include them in your written plan. Your plan should include:

- [ ] The time you will start the organized discussion.
- [ ] A reminder to pray before the lesson begins.
- [ ] The question numbers and whether you will cover, combine or skip them.
- [ ] The Bible verses you will read during the discussion
- [ ] What you will do for the application questions—large group, small group, or skip
- [ ] Extra research questions—mark whether you will include these in the discussion time or skip them.
- [ ] Any follow-up question(s) from your own study
- [ ] Write the time you will finish the lesson and end with prayer.

This is how you prepare wisely as the Content Guardian of your group.

WANT MORE IDEAS ON LEADING A SMALL GROUP?

Get "The 5 C's of Small Group Leadership" at melanienewton.com/small-group-leaders.

MELANIE NEWTON

SAMPLE LESSON LEADING PLAN

Everyday Women, Ever-Faithful God Bible Study

Lesson 2: Sarah — A Woman Like Us

Time Period: The Patriarchs ~2100-1800 B.C.

"Let your beauty not be external – the braiding of hair and wearing of gold jewelry or fine clothes – but the inner person of the heart, the lasting beauty of a gentle and tranquil spirit, which is precious in God's sight. For in the same way the holy women who hoped in God long ago adorned themselves by being subject to their husbands, like Sarah who obeyed Abraham, calling him lord. You become her children when you do what is good and have no fear in doing so." 1 PETER 3:3-6

Plan for Leading

(1½ to 2 Hour Session, 10:00-12:00)

Start at 10:05 with Get Acquainted question: *How long have you lived in this area? Where did you live before this?*

10:15 PRAY

Have someone read the Bible verse at top of page.

Ask if anyone has comments/questions on the Historical Perspective section.

Historical Perspective

The term *patriarch* denotes the father or male leader of a family or tribe. In the Bible, "patriarchs" usually refers to the three main characters in Genesis 12-50—Abraham, Isaac, and Jacob. Great civilizations dotted the Ancient Near East. Ur was a thriving city with efficient government and impressive buildings. Under God's direction, Abraham abandoned Ur, with its culture and conveniences, for the land of Canaan (today's Israel). Patriarchal life was semi-nomadic as they wandered from place to place, searching for grazing land and water for their animals. They measured their wealth in livestock and movable goods such as silver, gold, and tents.

Archeology has given rich insights into patriarchal times. In the early 1900's, Sir Leonard Woolley excavated Ur. He discovered the glory of the city, but he also recognized the sin. Idol worship characterized the city. It is little wonder that God called Abraham away.

The patriarchal era is important to us. Through Abraham and his descendants, God began to develop a people of His own. The Abrahamic Covenant (God's unconditional pledge to Abraham) contains many precious promises: Abraham would have numerous offspring; his descendants would possess the land of Canaan, and the Messiah would come forth one day from his line. These promises passed on to Isaac and Jacob. Jacob's sons formed the nucleus of the twelve tribes of Israel. Through one son's kindness (Joseph), the infant "Israel" (70+ people) entered Egypt and grew into a great nation.

SECTION 3: SAMPLE LESSON LEADING PLAN

DAY ONE STUDY

When we are introduced to this power couple in the history of Israel, their names are Abram and Sarai. For consistency's sake, we'll use the more common names "Abraham" and "Sarah" (names later given to them by God) throughout this lesson.

Moving from home (at 65 years old)

1. Read Genesis 11:27-12:9. Describe Sarah and her circumstances in life at this time.

2. ***Deeper Discoveries (optional):*** Research the city of Ur to find out what Sarah willingly left.

3. Barrenness for a woman in Sarah's time was very painful, not unlike for a woman in our time. Sons, in particular, were needed to carry on the family name and livelihood. How do you think Sarah's barrenness would have affected her feelings of security (particularly with Abraham) and significance (her status in society)?

4. Read Genesis 12:10-13:2. Why do you think Sarah went along with Abraham's "Tell them you're my sister" plan?

    Historical Insight: Curious about Abraham's "Tell them you're my sister" plan? One historian said that if a married man of Abraham's day found himself in enemy territory, he could be killed for his wife. But, if Abraham were known as her brother, someone wanting her would have to make marriage arrangements with Abram because in that society, a woman's brother gave his sister in marriage. So, Abraham would have been the negotiator thus giving him the chance to act in his own interest.

5. Consider how frightened Sarah might have been as she went along with Abraham's plan and was then taken into Pharaoh's harem. God honored Sarah for not giving way to that fear (1 Peter 3:5-6). When Abraham failed to protect Sarah in this incident, what did God do for her?

6. ***Your Life's Journey:***

    - Abraham had not given over the safety of his own life to the Lord yet because his faith did not extend to this area. What area of your life have you not fully given over to the Lord, and how does this affect those around you?

    - Sarah was ~65 when she left Haran, moving to who-knows-where, cooperating with God's plan for Abraham even when it was tough for her. How are you at encouraging your husband or your closest friend to follow God's leading?

Q1–Have someone read Genesis 11:27-12:9. Ask question. Several answers.

Q2–Ask if anyone did the research and wants to share

Q3–Ask question. Be sensitive to those with infertility.

Q4– Have someone read Genesis 12:10-13:2. Ask question.

Skip Historical Insight.

Q5–Ask question.

Q6–First question-large group ask for one person to share.

Second question-*Table Talk* in smaller groups. After 8 minutes, ask if anyone wants to share with the whole group.

SECTION 3: SAMPLE LESSON LEADING PLAN

DAY TWO STUDY

10 years later (Sarah is now ~75) ...

7. Read Genesis 15:1-6.

   - What was Abraham's "Plan B" to provide an heir?
   - What was still God's plan?
   - How many times had He told Abraham this already?

   Historical Insight: In ancient times, a man who had no son could adopt a favored servant as heir to his possessions. Or, a man who had no son could take a second wife to produce an heir. Some marriage contracts even spelled out this provision. A wife was obligated to have children. If she could not, she was required to find her husband another wife who could.

8. Read Genesis 16. This is Sarah's "Plan B" to fix Abraham's need for an heir. Discuss her idea and the emotions she might have experienced. Notice that Abraham had not already sought a second wife.

9. Sarah's "Plan B" becomes a nightmare! Our example was no perfect woman. She was just like we are. How did Sarah react?

10. What was threatened in Sarah's life, and what confirmation did she need from her husband?

    Scriptural Insight: Sin now drives a wedge between Hagar and Sarah. Hostility and mutual recrimination loom large, resulting in Hagar's fleeing her mistress's home precipitously, and pregnant at that. But in fleeing Sarah, several things happen to Hagar. She is the first person in the Bible to whom "the angel of the Lord" appears (16:11a). She is the first woman in the Bible to whom God directly makes a promise (16:11b-12). She is the only person in the Old Testament to give God a new name (16:13). And lastly, her meeting with the angel "is the only encounter between God and a woman that results in a commemorative place name (16:14)" (Adapted from Handbook on the Pentateuch, page 91)

13 years later (Sarah is now ~89)

11. Read Genesis 17:1-6, 15-22. God once again told Abraham His plan to provide descendants for Abraham and a faithful people for Himself.

    - How did Abraham respond this time?
    - What additional information is given in Romans 4:18-21?

12. Read Genesis 18:1-15. When the visitors came by Abraham's tent, what did the Lord give Sarah for the first time?

Q7–Have someone read Genesis 15:1-6. Ask questions.

Skip Historical Insight.

Q8–Read Genesis 16:1-6 only. Ask question.

Q9–Ask question.

Q10–Ask question.

Skip Scriptural Insight.

Q11– Have someone read Genesis 17:15-22. Ask the question.

Q12–Have someone read Genesis 18:6-15. Ask question.

Q13–Ask question.

SECTION 3: SAMPLE LESSON LEADING PLAN

13. What was Sarah's initial response? Why? [NOTE: The Hebrew word translated "pleasure" in verse 12 is *eden*, which is synonymous with sensual pleasure.]

14. Read Genesis 20. This happened shortly after the "tent" visit. Abraham nearly jeopardized the whole situation by again placing Sarah in another man's harem. He fails in the same area of faith in which he failed 25 years earlier (see Day One Study). At **89 years of age,** she was taken into a harem of the reigning king. (This gives further information regarding Sarah's beauty. God must have turned on her hormones again in a big way—super estrogen!!) There is no record that Sarah tried to protect herself this time or argue with Abraham. What does this tell you about her trust in both her husband and her God?

    Q14–Skip. Similar to earlier situation.

15. *Your Life's Journey:* Sarah loved Abraham for many years. She followed him in some very tough situations. Their life was definitely not static or boring. Just like ours.

    - If are married, in what areas have you learned greater trust of your husband?
    - If you are single, in what areas have you learned greater trust of a family member or close friend?

    Q15—Ask question and discuss as a large group rather than in *Table Talk*. OR Skip question if running out of time.

DAY THREE STUDY

16. Read Genesis 21:1-7. Describe Sarah's experience and the story she had to tell (vs. 6).

    Q16–Have someone read Genesis 21:1-7. Ask question.

    Think About It: Someone once said, "God's plan is completely different from what you could ever imagine and much more glorious than you would ever expect." Have you noticed this in your life? Is anything really too hard for the Lord?

    Have someone read "Think About It."

17. The name Isaac means "he laughs." In what ways is Isaac an appropriate name for this baby?

    Q17–Ask question.

18. Through this whole experience, how do we know that God loved Sarah as much as Abraham?

    Q18–Ask question. (I love this truth.)

3 YEARS LATER (SARAH IS NOW ~92)

19. Read Genesis 21:8-13. What situation existed between Abraham, Sarah, Hagar, and Ishmael?

    Q19–Have someone read Genesis 21:8-13. Ask question.

20. Contrast the response of Sarah with that of Abraham to the situation.

    Q20–Ask question.

21. Discuss God's response to the situation.

    Q21–Ask question.

22. Abraham needed Sarah's insight and advice in order to fulfill God's promise. Sometimes our husbands or closest friends need our advice. How should we pray concerning giving advice to them?

    Q22–Ask question.

SECTION 3: SAMPLE LESSON LEADING PLAN

23. Read Genesis 23:1-4, 16-20 and Genesis 25:1. Sarah lived to be 127 years old. What do you learn of Abraham's regard for her until death parted them?

    Q23–Ask question.

24. Read Hebrews 11:11-13. What testimony does the scripture give about Abraham and Sarah?

    Q24–Skip.

25. From our study, write down at least 7 descriptive characteristics of Sarah, positive or negative, that will help you to remember her.

    Q25–Ask question. Get several responses.

DAY FOUR STUDY — THE WALK FROM FEAR TO FAITH

God loved Sarah. He knew what was going on in her life. He was able to do something about it. But, God did not give Sarah a child early in her marriage nor did He prevent her from making a bad decision or spending time in a king's harem. During her walk, a loving God said "no" to some things. Yet, she chose to trust Him rather than submit to fear. And, God rewarded her faith with an outpouring of His blessing in other ways. Likewise, God may not choose to rescue you from poor decisions made by you or someone close to you. But, in any and all situations, you can count on these truths…

Read the paragraph and review the 4 truths together.

➢ God loves me.

➢ God knows what is going on in my life.

➢ God can do something about it.

➢ I can trust His goodness in whatever He chooses to do!

26. List all the situations in Sarah's life that could have "terrified" her.

27. Considering those "opportunities" for being terrified, in which ones did Sarah, by faith, do what was right and not give way to fear?

    Q26 & Q27 if time–Ask the question. Skip to make time for Q28.

28. **TELL YOUR STORY:** Sarah is commended by God for trusting in Him and not giving way to fear. In what areas of your life have you learned greater trust of your God?

    Q28–*Table Talk*: Give the women 10 minutes to share in their groups then ask if anyone wants to share with the whole group.

Read "God Is Bigger than Your Weaknesses" on the next page for additional insight to apply this lesson to your life.

Discuss Essay if time.

11:55 PRAY & reminder to do Lesson 3 for next time

SECTION 3: SAMPLE LESSON LEADING PLAN

WANT TO WORK THROUGH THIS SECOND LESSON?

Go to melanienewton.com/ot-women.

Section 4:

Lead Confidently as Content Guardian

MELANIE NEWTON

GUIDELINES FOR THE CONTENT GUARDIAN

Ask Jesus to help you with all of the following steps to leading a Bible study group. Depend on Him to show you what to do. He is faithful!

1. **START** at the time you said you would start with something: icebreaker, what jumped out at them in the lesson, or the first question.

2. **GUIDE** your small group into the living, transforming Word of God by opening and reading the Bible together in your small group.

3. **ENCOURAGE** everyone to discover God's Word on their own during the week, taking time to complete the lesson, and to share with each other what they have learned.

4. **WORK THROUGH** the questions by reading the question and waiting for the group respond.

5. **ASK**, "Anyone else?" for those questions requiring several answers until the ones you think are important have been shared.

6. **MOVE ON** after someone gives an answer for those questions requiring one answer.

7. **BE READY** if a question causes someone to get emotional. Put an arm around her, affirm her hurt, and pray for her. Then say, "Let's see how we can learn to trust God even in the midst of our hurt." Move on.

8. **COMMUNICATE ACCEPTANCE** in your eyes, manner, and your response to what a group member shares.

9. **AFFIRM** a woman after she shares, especially if she is normally quiet. Say, "Thank you for sharing that."

10. **CLARIFY** the truth should the comment need further explanation. Correct error gently if it is important to the discussion. Especially if what was said is not in the text. Always point them back to what the Scripture actually says.

11. **LIMIT** your own talking except to lead the discussion and to direct the discussion once it begins. Share your answers only when necessary or if something totally amazed you.

12. **AVOID** getting bogged down on any one issue. Pay attention to any notes you made about possible rabbit trails. Stay focused on what you decide is best for the group. Keep the discussion moving along.

13. **APPROACH THIS ROLE WITH HUMILITY AND GRACE.** Let them know that you are learning right alongside them. Be excited about what they see in the Scriptures as they study. Be amazed and humbled to hear someone else discover something in the passage that you missed.

This is how you lead wisely as the Content Guardian of your group.

SECTION 4: WORK THROUGH A LESSON

WANT MORE IDEAS ON LEADING A SMALL GROUP?

- Get "The 5 C's of Small Group Leadership" at melanienewton.com/small-group-leaders.

- Sign up for my e-course at melanienewton.com/courses. Get access to all the videos i offer to help you be the best bible study leader you can be.

MELANIE NEWTON

WORK THROUGH A LESSON

WORK THROUGH THIS LESSON FOR YOURSELF.

Everyday Women, Ever-Faithful God Bible Study

Lesson 3: Jochebed & Miriam — Influential Women

Time: The Exodus ~1450 B.C.

> *"For by the grace given to me I say to every one of you not to think more highly of yourself than you ought to think, but to think with sober discernment, as God has distributed to each of you a measure of faith. For just as in one body we have many members, and not all the members serve the same function, so we who are many are one body in Christ, and individually we are members who belong to one another."* ROMANS 12:3-5

Historical Perspective

For 430 years, Israelites lived in Egypt, at first in comfort because the "vice president" of the country was their relative Joseph. But after Joseph died, there arose a Pharaoh who did not know Joseph, and Israel's welcome grew cold. Fearing Israel's might, Egypt sought to cripple the growing nation. But Egypt's efforts were in vain; God was with His people, and He was preparing to bring Israel out of the land.

Conservative scholars date the "Exodus," a landmark in Israel's history, at 1446 B.C. Born shortly after the decree to throw Hebrew newborn boys in the Nile, Moses escaped death through adoption by pharaoh's daughter. About 1486, the reigning Pharaoh tried to kill Moses when he sought identity with his people Israel, but Moses escaped to Midian. Forty years later, the Lord appeared to Moses in a burning bush, and Moses returned to Egypt to stand before the Pharaoh of the exodus with his brother Aaron at his side.

Through Moses, God poured out His wrath upon Pharaoh and brought Egypt to her knees. Israel marched forth a free people, living proof of God's gracious salvation. Yet freedom did not guarantee success. Israel lacked organization. At Mount Sinai, God molded His people into a nation. The Mosaic Covenant governed every part of Israel's society: the civil, the ceremonial, and the moral. The covenant contained special promises, but it demanded obedience. Rebellion would bring severe judgment. Israel chose to rebel against her God. Sin brought judgment, and an entire generation died. Yet, God heard the prayers of Moses and preserved His people through the wilderness.

DAY ONE STUDY

Miriam's childhood and her mentors…

1. Read Exodus 1:1-2:10; Hebrews 11:23. Over several generations, God used brave women to thwart evil plans to eliminate His people. List the women mentioned in the Exodus passage who exhibited courage. These were Miriam's "mentors."

SECTION 4: WORK THROUGH A LESSON

2. From Exodus 6:20 and Numbers 26:59, we get additional information about Miriam's family. Her parents are named Amram and Jochebed. The children are Miriam, Aaron, and Moses. Read Hebrews 11:24-28. What influence, if any, did the few years spent with his parents have on Moses?

3. Back to Exodus 2:1-10, how would you describe Miriam's mom Jochebed to someone? In other words, what character qualities do you "see" in her?

4. What choices did Miriam's parents (Jochebed and Amram) make because of their faith, and how did God reward that faith?

5. Miriam had the same home and parents as Moses. From the Exodus 2:1-10 passage (she's the sister mentioned), use adjectives to describe Miriam who was 7-12 years of age at this time.

   From the Hebrew: Miriam's name in Hebrew means "bitterness." The Greek version of her name is Mary. In Israel's history after this time, Mary, Mara, and Miriam were popular girl's names.

6. As a young girl, then, what fearful situations did Miriam face, and how did she respond?

7. *Your Life's Journey:* Moses, Aaron and Miriam came from a home where parents were walking by faith in their God. In what kind of home did you grow up? How has this affected your ability to courageously trust God and not give way to fear?

DAY TWO STUDY

80 years later…

8. Read Exodus 14:1-31. Miriam is now in her upper mid-life, ~87-92 years old. What did she experience of God's faithfulness along with the rest of Israel?

SECTION 4: WORK THROUGH A LESSON

Scriptural Insight: According to tradition, Miriam was married to Hur, an honorable man who along with Aaron, held up Moses' arms during a major battle in Exodus 17:10-13. He was appointed magistrate while Moses was on the mountain (Ex. 24:14).

9. Read Exodus 15:1-21. What was Miriam's response to God's faithfulness?

10. Read Micah 6:3-4. What does God say about Miriam's role for Israel? In what ways is she pleasing God and fulfilling His purpose for her?

11. Why do you think Miriam's support would have been important to Moses?

12. Looking more closely at Exodus 15:20. What is Miriam called? Read Numbers 12:2. What does Miriam say about herself?

13. A prophetess was a female prophet—one to whom and through whom God speaks, revealing Himself and His will especially in the absence of the written word of God. God used a number of women to speak forth (prophesy) His Word at critical times in history. One was Deborah whom we'll be studying in an upcoming lesson. Another such woman was Huldah. Read 2 Kings 22:1-20. This occurred about 700 years after Miriam's time. What was going on, and how did Huldah serve God and the leader of Israel?

14. Prophesying also could involve an enthusiastic praising of God inspired by the Holy Spirit. Read 1 Samuel 10:5-10 and 1 Chronicles 25:1.

    - What activities were associated with prophesying?

    - In what ways does Exodus 15:20-21 fit this description of prophesying?

Scriptural Insight: The song in Exodus 15 is the first recorded song in the Bible—a song of redemption. Such celebration was common after victory in battle. Since the day of Pentecost, the Holy Spirit residing in believers continues to inspire enthusiastic praising of God. We don't call it prophesying any longer, but it still fits the biblical definition. The Holy Spirit inspires and gifts believers today to compose songs, poems, prayers and testimonies that glorify God.

SECTION 4: WORK THROUGH A LESSON

15. ***Your Life's Journey:*** The Holy Spirit still inspires us to break out in enthusiastic praise to God through various means. Have you written a song, a poem, prose, created a work of art, or simply sang praise songs to Him? What led to this expression in your life? You might want to respond to His faithfulness today with a "creative praise" expression in the space below. If you are in a small group, please consider sharing your "creative praise" with your group.

DAY THREE STUDY

About 2 years later…

16. Read Numbers 12:1-16. Why did Miriam and Aaron begin to talk against Moses?

17. What do you think was the real reason for their complaining?

> **Think About It**: One of the torments of envy is that it can never turn away its eyes from the thing that pains it. Envy blocks our trust in God, hurts our relationships, makes us resent God's goodness to others, and blinds us to God's goodness to us.

18. Discuss the Lord's response to their behavior (vs. 2-9).

19. What is implied by the fact that the Lord punished only Miriam? See also James 3:5-6.

> **Scriptural Insight:** Spitting in one's face expressed contempt (Deut. 25:9). The Lord expressed His contempt for Miriam's presumption by the skin affliction.

SECTION 4: WORK THROUGH A LESSON

20. Why was a skin disease such as leprosy so awful? See Numbers 5:1-4.

Think About It: Miriam bucked her authority, claiming equal prominence with Moses. Because of her attitude and resulting action, God disciplined her through banishment, opposite of what she really wanted!

21. How did Miriam's brothers respond to the discipline of their sister?

22. Read Deuteronomy 24:8-9. What do you think was the effect of Miriam's banishment from the camp for 7 days…

    - on her?
    - on the people?

Historical Insight: Sometimes Miriam was a good example; sometimes a bad example. Just like we are, she was not perfect every day. Yet, she had been given a sphere of influence by God. She lived through 38 years of wandering and died just before Aaron in the 40th year out of Egypt at ~130 years old (Numbers 20:1).

23. Read Romans 13:1-2 and Hebrews 13:7,17. How does what you read in Numbers 12 illustrate these passages?

24. *Your Life's Journey:* There are serious consequences of our attitudes towards authority.

    - Though all of us are not leaders, all of us are under some kind of authority in the Church. Is there someone in leadership now of whom you are jealous, resentful, or disapproving? Do you try to undermine their leadership by gossip or slander? Read Proverbs 10:19. Discuss how to apply this scripture to your life.

    - Read Mark 10:42-45, Galatians 5:26, Philippians 2:3-4, Romans 12:3-5, and 1 Peter 5:1-5. These verses, teaching how we should all relate to each other in God's family, apply as well to leaders. What attitudes should we have if we are in leadership positions in the Body of Christ?

SECTION 4: WORK THROUGH A LESSON

DAY FOUR STUDY — THE WALK FROM FEAR TO FAITH

God loved Miriam's family. He knew what was going on in their lives. He was able to do something about it. But, God did not give Jochebed her son back permanently to raise nor did He prevent them from having to go through the agony of hiding baby Moses. Miriam was given great responsibility and privilege, yet she also had to live with the consequences of her sin. During her walk, a loving God said "no" to some things. Yet, Miriam and her family chose to trust Him rather than submit to fear. And, God rewarded their faith with an outpouring of His blessing in other ways. Likewise, God may not choose to rescue you from your "Egypt." But, in any and all situations, you can count on these truths…

- ➢ God loves me.
- ➢ God knows what is going on in my life.
- ➢ God can do something about it.
- ➢ I can trust His goodness in whatever He chooses to do!

25. What situations could have caused fear for Jochebed? How did she respond to God by faith?

26. Thinking back through Miriam's life, what situations did she face that could have terrified her? How did she respond to God by faith in those situations?

27. **TELL YOUR STORY:** Jesus had a testimony to share. He said in John 8:14, "Even if I testify on my own behalf, my testimony is valid, for I know where I came from and where I am going. But you have no idea where I come from or where I am going." What He said about Himself was His STORY. Miriam testified about God's faithfulness through her use of poetry, song, and dance. Even if you've never testified like Miriam did, your STORY of God's faithfulness in your life is your testimony about Him. Write a short paragraph telling of an area in your life where you have recognized God's faithfulness to you. This is a part of your STORY of God's faithfulness.

NOW USE THE "LESSON LEADING CHECKLIST" FROM SECTION THREE TO REVIEW THIS LESSON AND MAKE YOUR PLAN ON THE "LESSON PLAN WORKSHEET" ON THE NEXT PAGE.

MELANIE NEWTON

LESSON PLAN WORKSHEET

Ask Jesus to help you make and follow a plan for leading a Bible study group. Depend on Him to show you what to do. He is faithful!

_____ START TIME

_____ PRAY

Q	Q
Q	Q
Q	Q
Q	Q
Q	Q
Q	Q
Q	Q
Q	Q
Q	Q
Q	Q
Q	Q
Q	Q
Q	Q
Q	Q
Q	Q

_____ PRAY

SECTION 4: LESSON PLAN WORKSHEET

Ask Jesus to help you make and follow a plan for leading a Bible study group. Depend on Him to show you what to do. He is faithful!

_____ Start Time

_____ Pray

Q	Q
Q	Q
Q	Q
Q	Q
Q	Q
Q	Q
Q	Q
Q	Q
Q	Q
Q	Q
Q	Q
Q	Q
Q	Q
Q	Q
Q	Q

_____ Pray

Section 5:

Lead Graciously as Community Builder

MELANIE NEWTON

COMMON CHALLENGES WORKSHEET

Ask Jesus to help you with all of the following challenges to leading a Bible study group. Depend on Him to show you what to do. He is faithful!

Let your conversation be always full of grace, seasoned with salt, so that you may know how to answer everyone. (Colossians 4:6)

Let's look at some of the most common challenges that both experienced and new leaders face and gracious, loving ways to respond to those challenges. Learn how to *Lead Graciously as a Community Builder*. And, trust in Jesus to help you do this.

Challenge #1: Encouraging everyone to participate in the discussion

- It's not your job to make everyone talk.
- Try to offer small groups of 2-4 people to discuss some questions.
- Avoid calling on people to make them participate.
- Listen well and affirm answers.

Your ideas or experience:

Challenge #2: Managing talkative people so they don't dominate the discussion

- If you are the talkative one, mark the question(s) where you want to share an answer. Otherwise, let the rest of the group members answer the questions.
- Pray for Jesus to help you think of words you can use to jump in and sum up what they just said. Use humor.
- Quickly thank them for an answer, turn your eyes away, and move on.
- If you have people who know they talk too much in your group, talk with them outside of class and let them know that you would like them to keep their answers shorter. Work out a signal between the two of you when she is talking too much. If you do it graciously, most people will respond just fine.
- Remember you are the Content Guardian. The group depends on you to do this. So, don't let the talkative people dominate your group.

Your ideas or experience:

SECTION 5: COMMON CHALLENGES WORKSHEET

Challenge #3: Choosing a Bible study that everyone likes

- Fact: you won't be able to please everyone. Therefore, don't even open it up to the group for a choice.
- Pray about what is best for the group.
- Choose what interests you, where you would like to grow in your faith. If you are passionate about what you are studying, that will be infectious to the rest of the group.
- For those who might have already studied that book of the Bible you chose,
  - Suggest to them that this might be the time when they help someone else understand it.
  - Remind them that Bible study in a group is not all about "me." It's about the whole group learning together.
  - The Word of God is alive and active. If she is open to it, she will learn something new.
- If someone who has been in Bible studies for years complains that the one you chose is too easy,
  - Suggest that they invite a friend or co-worker who is new to the Bible to attend this one. Then, he or she can be the mentor for that person.

Your ideas or experience:

Challenge #4: Feeling overwhelmed with the responsibility

- Ask someone in the group to be your helper with the organizational stuff.
- If your group is large enough, ask someone to be your co-leader so that she would be prepared with her lesson to step in if something happened to you one day.
  - It is always good to have someone else take ownership of the group besides you. And, it gives experience to someone else in leading a group.
  - You can give her your plan or suggest she make her own.
  - If two of you are co-leading a group, you can let the one who is most comfortable leading the discussion fill the role of Content Guardian and the one who is best at organizing or connecting with the women fill the role of Community Builder
- Ask outgoing women to help with making others feel connected to the group

Your ideas or experience:

SECTION 5: COMMON CHALLENGES WORKSHEET

Challenge #5: Afraid you don't know the answers

- Assume you will get asked questions for which you don't know the answers.
- Remember your role is Content Guardian. Stay focused on the lesson.
- Dwell on what you can know. Avoid speculation just to come up with an answer.
- Humbly accept what you can't know or don't understand.

Your ideas or experience:

Challenge #6: Getting nervous speaking in front of people

- Practice speaking through your plan. I do that still, after all these years.
- Read the questions aloud and how you will ask someone to read the Bible verses.
- Practice explaining how you will do the application questions if you choose to do any in smaller groups.
- Put notes in strategic places in the lesson where you need some extra reminding of details. I do this, too.
- Practice how you will respond to potential rabbit trails or challenging questions. Do this with a smile. Remember to not act shocked.

Your ideas or experience:

Challenge #7: Some aren't doing their lessons ahead of time

- You can't control this. Don't let it annoy you. Encourage them to come to the study and learn as you read the Bible passages and discuss them together.
- Realize that some people are so busy with work, school, and family, that they have a hard time finding extra time to do another thing for themselves. It could be just the season of life.
- Keep encouraging them to feed themselves from God's Word, even if they only do the first page of the lesson. Do something.
- If this is the majority of your group, pick a shorter Bible study that can be done in one sitting.

Your ideas or experience:

SECTION 5: COMMON CHALLENGES WORKSHEET

Challenge #8: The temptation to "fix" each other's problems

- Don't let this happen. It is not the group's job to fix each other. That belongs to Jesus.
- Tell them up front, "We are not going to try to fix each other's issues. We will be good listeners."
- As the leader, point everyone to depend on Jesus to show them a way out of any challenge.
- Say, "When you share your lives and how Jesus has helped you, the others in the group will hear that. If they want to ask you questions about it, get together with them later."

Your ideas or experience:

Challenge #9: When group members drop out

- Don't take it personally. Give any feelings of insecurity to Jesus!
- Some sign up for a Bible study group with good intentions of doing the lessons and attending regularly. But, things get in the way.
- Try to find out the reasons why. More than likely it's not your leadership but that person's season of life. Or, their schedule has changed preventing them from continuing.
- If you have newcomers to your group, or those who don't already feel connected, make an effort to connect with them personally. I find that if I connect with someone who kinda stays on the "fringe" or outside of the group, there is a higher likelihood that they will continue to try out the group. Then, we have a better chance to connect her with the other group members.
- Ask a trusted friend to let you know if your leadership style might be pushing someone away. Like I have mentioned several times, be humble and gracious in your role as Content Guardian.
- If there is anything you can address with her or with the group to keep her coming, do that. Otherwise, just let it go.

Your ideas or experience:

FOR MORE IDEAS ON LEADING A SMALL GROUP & RESPONDING TO CHALLENGES,

- Get "The 5 C's of Small Group Leadership" at melanienewton.com/small-group-leaders.

- Sign up for my e-course at melanienewton.com/courses. Get access to all the videos I offer to help you be the best bible study leader you can be.

MELANIE NEWTON

Enjoy the Adventure

Thank you for joining me in this course, *Bible Study Leadership Made Easy.* You have learned a lot. Now, you are ready to enjoy the adventure as you step out in faith to lead a Bible study next week, next month, or next year.

If you are still feeling inadequate to lead a Bible study, everyone feels that way when they are just starting out leading a study. You are not alone in how you feel. It's okay to feel a bit scared. Remember why? Who makes you able to lead a Bible study? Jesus does!

As Paul wrote in Colossians 1,

> *He is the one we proclaim, admonishing and teaching everyone with all wisdom, so that we may present everyone fully mature in Christ. To this end I strenuously contend with **all the energy Christ so powerfully works in me**. (Colossians 1:28-29)*

When you are scared, you will rely on His power more. He will give you the confidence and grace to keep going. It's okay to say, "Lord, I'm nervous. I feel like I don't know enough. I know I can't do this alone. I will trust you to do this in me and through me." Watch what He does!

You have access to this course for as long as you need it. Just log in with your password each time and review.

PLEASE GO TO MELANIENEWTON.COM AND SIGN UP FOR MY *JOYFUL WALK MINISTRIES* NEWSLETTER. YOU WILL GET EASY ACCESS TO ALL THE FREE RESOURCES ON MY WEBSITE.

If you use a Joyful Walk Bible Study for yourself or your group, please write a review on Amazon for me.

ENJOY THE ADVENTURE

May Jesus make your time as a Bible Study leader very fruitful for Him. Enjoy the blessings of discovering God's Word together with a group of people and watch each one experience a joyful walk with Jesus. It will be a great adventure!

WAS THIS COURSE HELPFUL?

Please share about "Bible Study Leadership Made Easy" on Facebook, Twitter, Instagram, LinkedIn and more places so that others can learn how to lead a Bible Study with confidence & grace, too.

MELANIE NEWTON
RESOURCES PAGE

BIBLE STUDY NOTES FOR EVERY BOOK
http://www.soniclight.com/

BIBLE GATEWAY (MANY TRANSLATIONS OF THE BIBLE)
https://www.biblegateway.com/

BLUE LETTER BIBLE (TRANSLATION COMPARISONS AND OTHER STUDY TOOLS)
https://www.blueletterbible.org/

VINES EXPOSITORY DICTIONARY FOR NEW TESTAMENT WORDS
https://www.studylight.org/dictionaries/ved.html

INTERLINEAR BIBLE – GREEK AND HEBREW WITH CONCORDANCE
http://www.biblestudytools.com/interlinear-bible/

GOT QUESTIONS? (ANSWERS TO THE MOST COMMON QUESTIONS ABOUT THE BIBLE)
https://www.gotquestions.org/

PROBE MINISTRIES (APOLOGETICS AND CULTURE)
http://www.probe.org/

ENJOY THE ADVENTURE

BIBLE STUDIES BY MELANIE NEWTON

Graceful Beginnings Series books for new-to-the-Bible Christians:
- *A Fresh Start*
- *Painting the Portrait of Jesus*
- *The God You Can Know*
- *Grace Overflowing*
- *The Walk from Fear to Faith*
- *Satisfied by His Love*

Joyful Walk Bible Studies for growing Christians:
- *Graceful Living: The Essentials of Living a Grace-Based Christian Life*
- *7 Cs of a Firm Foundation: A Study Based on Genesis 1-11*
- *Everyday Women, Ever Faithful God: Old Testament Women*
- *Profiles of Perseverance: Old Testament Men*
- *Live Out His Love: New Testament Women*
- *Radical Acts: Adventure with the Spirit from the Book of Acts*
- *Knowing Jesus, Knowing Joy: A Study of Philippians*
- *Healthy Living: A Study of Colossians*
- *Adorn Yourself with Godliness: A Study of 1 Timothy and Titus*
- *Perspective: A Study of 1 and 2 Thessalonians*
- *To Be Found Faithful: A Study of 2 Timothy*

Find these and more resources for your spiritual growth at melanienewton.com.

Made in the USA
Lexington, KY
26 May 2018